ALSO BY JUDITH VIORST

POEMS

The Village Square

It's Hard to Be Hip Over Thirty and Other Tragedies of Married Life

People and Other Aggravations

How Did I Get to Be Forty and Other Atrocities

If I Were in Charge of the World and Other Worries

Forever Fifty and Other Negotiations

Sad Underwear and Other Complications

Suddenly Sixty and Other Shocks of Later Life

I'm Too Young to Be Seventy and Other Delusions

Unexpectedly Eighty and Other Adaptations

*Wait for Me and Other Poems About the Irritations
and Consolations of a Long Marriage*

What Are You Glad About? What Are You Mad About?

CHILDREN'S BOOKS

Sunday Morning

I'll Fix Anthony

Try It Again, Sam

The Tenth Good Thing About Barney

Alexander and the Terrible, Horrible, No Good, Very Bad Day

*My Mama Says There Aren't Any Zombies, Ghosts, Vampires, Creatures, Demons, Monsters,
Fiends, Goblins, or Things*

Rosie and Michael

Alexander, Who Used to Be Rich Last Sunday

The Good-bye Book

Earrings!

The Alphabet From Z to A (With Much Confusion on the Way)

Alexander, Who's Not (Do You Hear Me? I Mean It!) Going to Move

Absolutely Positively Alexander

Super-Completely and Totally the Messiest!

Just in Case

Nobody Here but Me

Lulu and the Brontosaurus

Lulu Walks the Dogs

Lulu's Mysterious Mission

Alexander, Who's Trying His Best to Be the Best Boy Ever

And Two Boys Booed

Lulu Is Getting a Sister (Who Wants Her? Who Needs Her?)

OTHER

Yes, Married

A Visit from St. Nicholas (To a Liberated Household)

Love & Guilt & the Meaning of Life, Etc.

Necessary Losses

Murdering Mr. Monti

Imperfect Control

You're Officially a Grown-Up

Grown-Up Marriage

Alexander and the Wonderful, Marvelous, Excellent, Terrific Ninety Days

Nearing Ninety

and

Other Comedies of Late Life

Judith Viorst

Illustrated by Laura Gibson

Simon & Schuster

NEW YORK   LONDON   TORONTO   SYDNEY   NEW DELHI

Simon & Schuster
1230 Avenue of the Americas
New York, NY 10020

First Simon & Schuster hardcover edition April 2019

SIMON & SCHUSTER and colophon are registered trademarks of Simon & Schuster, Inc.

For information about special discounts for bulk purchases, please contact Simon & Schuster Special Sales
at 1-866-506-1949 or business@simonandschuster.com.

The Simon & Schuster Speakers Bureau can bring authors to your live event. For more information or to book an event,
contact the Simon & Schuster Speakers Bureau at 1-866-248-3049 or visit our website at www.simonspeakers.com.

Interior design by Ruth Lee-Mui

Manufactured in the United States of America

1   3   5   7   9   10   8   6   4   2

Library of Congress Cataloging-in-Publication Data
Names: Viorst, Judith, author.
Title: Nearing ninety : and other comedies of late life / Judith Viorst.
Description: New York : Simon & Schuster, 2019.
Identifiers: LCCN 2018041924 (print) | LCCN 2018042860 (ebook) | ISBN
9781501197123 (Ebook) | ISBN 9781501197086 (hardback)
Subjects: | BISAC: HUMOR / Form / Limericks & Verse. | HUMOR / Topic /
Relationships. | POETRY / American / General.
Classification: LCC PS3572.I6 (ebook) | LCC PS3572.I6 A6 2019 (print) |
DDC 811/.54—dc23
LC record available at https://urldefense.proofpoint.com/v2/url?u=https-3A__lccn.loc.gov_2
018041924&d=DwIFAg&c=jGUuvAdBXp_VqQ6t0yah2g&r=7Powweyp97H7BrdRqAm-
eJjycEUd2REgi140E_-eJsoFHotHpuSHVST6CEgk6PFC&m=xa7gcRMBCh8w8YJNI1AwuIsV
NZC2-sov5CkNuSlAnzo&s=DUgh8XBvOl1eBfM_fsa-DmCar5N_oxhU_pMNPOr-Dlk&e=

ISBN 978-1-5011-9708-6
ISBN 978-1-5011-9712-3 (ebook)

In memory of Robert Pitofsky, beloved friend

To be interested in the changing seasons is a happier state of mind than to be hopelessly in love with spring.
—George Santayana

Contents

xi

Sightings 27

Endings 49

Ninety

What Happened

Tell me, what is it you plan to do with your one wild and precious life?
—MARY OLIVER

So while I was writing thank-you notes for the guest towels, the fondue
forks, and the other wedding presents;
And while I was mastering Julia's *coq au vin*;
And while I was discovering that I had married a man who didn't believe in
entering checks in a checkbook;
And while we were disagreeing about the cost of the couch, the color of the
kitchen, being late, and the frequency of sex;
And while we were having babies who immediately transformed us into
besotted parents and sleep-deprived wrecks;
(So much for sex);

And while I was doing carpools in station wagons and polyester, while
    beaded, bell-bottomed swingers were having a ball;
And while I was being wifely, maternal, professional, and political and
    wondering what was so great about having it all;
And while he was asking would it really kill me to be nice to his cousin
    Arnie, to which my honest answer was yes it would;
And while I was asking whether, when he went overnight to Boston and
    didn't phone me, he was up to his ears in work—or up to no good;
And while I was going through my what's-the-meaning-of-it-all-after-all
    midlife crisis, resolved with some therapy and an eyelid lift;
And while we were deciding if we were ready to make the shift from ski
    vacations to Caribbean cruises;
And while, when the children were grown up and gone, and he had finally
    retired, and we were—for better or worse—alone at last;
And while, as the years sped past, we found ourselves listening to more
    eulogies than symphonies;
And while I drove him to specialists and he drove me to specialists and
    we kept each other warm when it was cold,
What happened was we got oldish, then older, then even older than that.
And then we got old.

Trading Places

All women become like their mothers.
—OSCAR WILDE

You can't read the menu if you don't bring your glasses.
Nor will your hearing aid work with a dead battery.
I once had these conversations with my mother.
Now my kids are having them with me.

You only should come if you want to come—no pressure.
You've got your own life to live. Go live it! Have fun!
That's how my mother used to get me to visit.
I can't believe that's what I just said to my son.

It's Time

One must work with time and not against it.
—URSULA K. LE GUIN

It's time that I gave up showing a little cleavage.
It's time that he wore his shirts out instead of tucked in.
It's time, whenever we tell a joke, that before we even
    begin,
We should first make sure we still remember the punch line.

It's time I got rid of that treadmill I'm not treading.
It's time he got over believing that he still skis.
And given the current condition of his lower back and my
    knees,
It's time we quit doing the Lindy Hop at weddings.

It's time that I found a bathing-suit alternative.
It's time, when offered a seat on the bus, he says yes.
It's time we stopped eating at restaurants where no one can hear,
    unless
We go on a night we're not talking to each other.

It's time for us to renew our opera subscription.
It's time to renew our subscription to the ballet.
But given that we should be working with time and not the other
    way,
And given we're not as perky at night as earlier in the day,
And given we've snoozed through many a Mimi and many a
    plié,
We'll be switching to matinees because . . . it's time.

Still Kissing After All These Years

Give me a thousand kisses, then another hundred,
then another thousand, then a second hundred. . . .
—GAIUS VALERIUS CATULLUS

All I can tell you about what marital bliss is
Is that I'm still a fool for my husband's kisses:
Hello kisses.
Good-bye kisses.
Lingering kisses.
Cursory kisses.
Private kisses.
Public kisses.
Make-out kisses.
Make-up kisses.
Good-night kisses.
Mid-night kisses,
And even before-he-brushes-his-teeth-in-the-
Morning kisses.
So whatever it is he's doing, he's done it just fine
Since that very first kiss back in 1949.

I Should Be Over This By Now

Have you ever noticed that *stressed* is *desserts* spelled backwards?
—ANONYMOUS

Though the state of the world,
The well-being of my children,
And whether my husband and I are doing okay,
Determine how contented I'm feeling
On a given day,
So, I'm ashamed to admit,
Does . . . how much I weigh.

I surely should be over this by now,
Considering that I'm a woman who holds decent values
On matters like peace and justice and human rights,
And therefore should not be obsessing
Over the utterly trivial fact that
My thighs are straining against the seams of my tights,
Which they wouldn't if I weighed what I wanted to weigh.

I certainly should be over this by now,
Considering that I'm a woman of some substance,
Acquainted with symphonies, sonnets, and Socrates,
And therefore shouldn't be troubled
By the inconsequential fact that
My stomach tends to obscure a clear view of my knees,
Which it wouldn't if I weighed what I wanted to weigh.

I definitely should be over this by now.

But I'm still denying myself the pleasures of eating.
I'm still pureeing potions of yogurt and kale.
I'm still abjuring chocolate (except when I'm cheating).
I'm still buying every damn diet book that's for sale.
And I'm still getting up, pulse racing, every morning
To read the day's verdict on my bathroom scale,
When I really should be over this by now.

Dealing With It

What counts in making a happy marriage is not
so much how compatible you are, but how you
deal with incompatibility.

—LEO TOLSTOY

When should a husband confess that he had an affair? (1)
How long should a wife feel entitled to hold a grudge? (2)
What's he to say when he hates what she's done with her hair? (3)
What's she to do when, though totally wrong, he won't budge? (4)
How does a wife get her husband to take all his pills? (5)
Is ninety too old to have sex in the back of a van? (6)
What's to be done with each other's diminishing skills? (7)
Is she the right woman for him? Is he the right man? (8)

(1) Probably never.
(2) Maybe forever.
(3) How about lying?
(4) There's always crying.
(5) Don't be a pest.
(6) Surely you jest.
(7) Simplify stuff.
(8) Right enough! Right enough!

The New Year's Eve Party

I love such mirth as does not make friends ashamed
to look upon one another next morning.
—IZAAK WALTON

For decades we have gathered together
Every New Year's Eve, at our all-dressed-up party,
Eight couples—now five couples, two widows, one widower,
Who have managed to make it through another year
Of the usual and not-so-usual calamities,
So that here we are again, in serious suits and high-ish heels,
Exchanging photographs and diagnoses,
Sharing joys, anxieties, and hugs,
Observing in each other the steady slippage of body, of mind,
        of champagne consumption,
And fighting off, in spite of our afternoon naps,
An almost overwhelming need for sleep,
But insistently hanging in there, every one of us,
Chatting and smiling and sipping and . . . hanging in,
Till the clock strikes twelve, the ball drops, we trade kisses
        all around,
And—finally! at last! thank God!—we can go home.

On Nearing Ninety

I'm still here.
—STEPHEN SONDHEIM

Old age: the crown of life . . .
—MARCUS TULLIUS CICERO

I'm past my sell-by date.
I hate to contemplate
That soon self-driving cars will rule the road.
My social network skills
Are whatever less than nil is.
And I still can't set my phone on airplane mode

This world of drone and bot
Confuses me a lot.
The Next Big Thing will just make me perspire.
Ambition's ship has sailed.
And I rarely get derailed
By fervid fantasies of wild desire.

But life's crown is old age,
So I won't slink off the stage.
Although not always with-it, I'm still here.
And since I plan to stay,
The role I hope to play
Is Queen Elizabeth—it's not King Lear.

In Praise of the Double Bed

What a happy and holy fashion it is that those who love
one another should rest on the same pillow.

—NATHANIEL HAWTHORNE

Waking up at my age
Is already an achievement,
Having finally fallen asleep with assorted pains, palpitations,
     and other precursors of doom
That for yet another day have proven not fatal.

My gummy eyes peer anxiously at the blurry numbers of the
     bedside clock,
Straining, without my glasses, to determine
If it's a sufficient 7:20 a.m., or merely a miserable 25 to 4,
Which is too late for Ambien—and too soon to get up.

My husband, lying beside me,
Snorts, stirs, sinks back into slumber,
While I mobilize to climb out of our high double bed,
Our old-fashioned brass double bed, so small in contrast to
     the copious, sprawling King Size,
But making it possible, over long decades of marriage,
For many a marital quarrel to be resolved

By a knee (accidentally) bumping against a thigh,
By a hand (accidentally) brushing across a breast,
By a toenail (accidentally) scraping a shin,
Because there's not enough room in a double bed
To fully retreat to "my" side and to "his" side,
And because, though angry back turns to angry back,
Our tushies will inevitably make contact
As we try—and fail—to sulk the night away.

Telling My Age

The woman who tells her age is either too young to have anything to lose or too old to have anything to gain.
—CHINESE PROVERB

I used to really enjoy telling people my age
For the shameless pleasure of hearing everyone say,
"You're kidding!"
"I don't believe it!"
"That's amazing!"
"I'm fainting with shock!"
Plus allusions to *The Picture of Dorian Gray*.
But now that no one is fainting
Or thinking I'm kidding
Or being amazed
Or insisting that what I'm saying
Couldn't be true,
I'm done
I'm finished
It's over
Forget about it
I am through
With telling my age.

What We Still Argue About

I'm not arguing. I'm simply explaining why I'm right.
—T-SHIRT

He thinks he can read *The New York Times* and still give me his undivided
   attention.
He only says that I look good when I stand in front of him asking, "So how
   do I look?"
He continues to claim, despite compelling evidence to the contrary, that his
   mother was actually an excellent cook.
And when he's telling a story he shouldn't be telling and I'm kicking him
   under the table,
He doesn't shut up. He hollers, "Why are you kicking me?"

He doesn't believe that leftovers should be subject to any statute of
   limitations.
He doesn't believe that reading the directions might help him to figure out
   how to work the remote.
He cannot resist correcting me every single time I mispronounce a word or
   mess up a quote.
And when I'm gently suggesting that he probably would prefer to *not* run
   over that mother and child in the crosswalk,
You wouldn't believe what he says about my suggestion.

He's hot when I'm cold and cold when I'm hot. We continue to be
thermostatically incompatible.
I turn the lights on. He turns the lights off. If I break a hip in the dark it
will be on his head.
And if there should be an Afterlife, we'll still be having arguments after
we're dead,
Because one of us—I'm not naming names—is more difficult than the
other of us, and besides,
What would a marriage be like with nothing to argue about?

Right Now

Happiness . . . not in another place but this place,
not for another hour but this hour.

—WALT WHITMAN

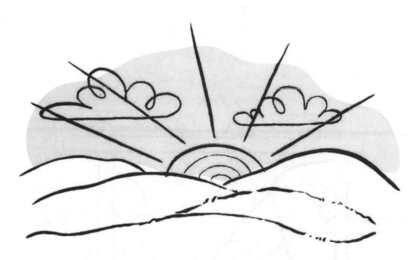

Right now
I'm not really thinking that
My knee replacement needs a knee replacement,
Or my grandson might actually marry that awful girl,
Or maybe it's time to switch from stocks to gold bars.

Right now
I'm not really thinking about
Comparative retirement communities,
Or the speed at which the polar ice caps are melting,
Or why they're letting people our age still drive cars.

Right now
I'm not resenting the fact
That I'm wide-awake this early in the morning
After yet another insomniac night,
Because, outside my bedroom window, streams of rosy light
Are slowly spilling across the undarkening sky,
While the sun blazes into being at the horizon.
And there's nothing else to think about,
Nothing else to know,
Nothing else I need to know
Right now.

Sightings

Man Mowing the Grass

I learned to observe the world around me,
and to note what I saw.

—MARGARET MEAD

Maybe you haven't noticed that bare-chested fellow,
That flat-bellied, slim-waisted fellow mowing the grass,
The one with the black curly hair, and the tattooed shoulder,
And the low-slung blue jeans lovingly molding his ass.
He's bobbing his head to the music that streams through his earbuds.
He's mouthing the words to some seethingly sensual song.
You think I'm out here on the porch just reading my novel?
You are so wrong.

The Graduation Brunch

There's
The vegan.
The vegetarian.
The kosher.
The gluten-free.
The one who's allergic to peanuts.
The one who's allergic to shellfish.
And the one who shouldn't be sitting next to her former husband's
      wife,
Who shouldn't be sitting next to her husband's ex-in-laws.

There's also
The one on antidepressants.
The one on probation.
The hyperactive twins, whose parents were told no kids were invited
      but brought them anyway.
The cousin who's suing his cousin over a real-estate deal gone bad.
The cousin who is countersuing that cousin.
The aunt describing in vivid detail her hernia operations to the uncle
      with plenty to say about his prostate.

And the graduate, who's on the back porch, ingesting something he
shouldn't be ingesting.

There's also
The one who converses only with his iPhone.
The one who converses only about the Dow.
The one in recovery, sharing her life story.
The one in roofing, handing out business cards.
The sister who's conspicuously engaged in make-out activities with
her new girlfriend.
The brother who's calling everyone who didn't vote for his candidate
morally bankrupt.
The mystery guest, who has finished his fourth Bloody Mary and
is working his way through his seventh mini quiche.
And the grandparents of the graduate, who are old enough to know
That the only response to all of this is . . . rejoice.

In the Park

... and how many times can a man turn his head
And pretend that he just doesn't see?
—BOB DYLAN

Raggedy Andy and Raggedy Ann
Are enjoying the day as best they can,
Sunning themselves on a bench in the park
With nowhere to go when it starts turning dark.

Once they perhaps were a source of great joy,
Somebody's dear little girl, little boy.
But stumbles and fumbles turned into a rout,
And all of their stuffing began to fall out.

Did they lack backbone, grit, courage, and pluck?
Or is it simply that I got the luck
That allows me to hand them some change and be done
With raggedy folks on a bench in the sun.

The Crestwood Village Retirement Community

New beginnings are often disguised as painful endings.

—LAO TZU

He is trying not to think of his new home as death's waiting room,
But now and then the phrase leaps into his mind,
Despite how alert and charming and attractive his fellow (inmates?)
    residents seem
When encountered at the exercise class, the swimming pool, the book
    group, the dining hall,
Or at any of the many other well-attended offerings of
The Crestwood Village Retirement Community,
To which he has retired, having lost his wife, sold his house,
And practiced triage on a lifetime of treasured possessions
In order to be able to fit his (diminished?) uncluttered self
Into a handsome, sunlit, two-bedroom apartment
In the popular Independent Living Unit of
The Crestwood Village Retirement Community,
Which also, somewhere, in another building,
Houses all of its less-than-lively residents,
Who have moved from Independent to . . . Assisted . . . Continuous . . .
    Urgent . . . Final Care,
And who'll never again be encountered at the exercise class, pool,
    book group, or dining hall,
Where, dressed in a natty blue blazer and making friends to his left
    and his right,
He is thinking that if this is—indeed—death's waiting room,
Death is damn well going to have to wait.

Charlie Beerman

Dogs do speak, but only to those who
know how to listen.
—ORHAN PAMUK

I don't do dogs, I explain to Charlie Beerman,
A springer spaniel who won't take no for an answer,
And who, whenever I visit the house where he lives,
Sits at my feet and rests his chin on my knee,
Gazing into my eyes with moist devotion
For ten or fifteen or twenty patient moments,
While I again explain that I don't do dogs,
Until he again persuades me that I do.

The Babes of the
Upper East Side

. . . today there are parts of Manhattan . . . where there
are no gray-haired women at all.
—NORA EPHRON

Though I haven't owned a belt since I was forty,
Preferring clothes that don't require a waist,
I'm nicely turned out, whether gowned or sporty,
And don't feel like a schlump unless I'm faced
With a height of perfection that makes me want to hide,
Displayed by the beauteous babes of the Upper East Side.

They tap along on five-inch Jimmy Chooses
With sculpted cheekbones, artfully streaked hair,
Impeccable from sunglasses to shoeses
And dressed in ways the rest of us don't dare.
And whatever their age, it can plausibly be denied
By these ageless, unblemished babes of the Upper East Side.

While elsewhere, over time, folks tend to fatten,
A fact of life I've frequently bemoaned,
The skinny rule in this part of Manhattan,
Where everybody's body's taut and toned,
And no upper-arm flab or posterior droop ever spied
On the iron-pumped, glute-tightened babes of the Upper East Side.

What has become of all the other ladies,
The ones who look a lot like you and me?
Perhaps they've all been shipped to the West Eighties.
Perhaps they've moved to Washington, D.C.,
Or wherever the softened and sagging can safely reside
Far from those high-fashion, flat-bellied, size-zero, flawless,
        and fabulous babes of the Upper East Side.

At the Nursing Home

Touch me,
remind me who I am.
—STANLEY KUNITZ

She gets on the crowded crosstown bus
To visit him once a day,
Though there's never a seat
And people push and shove you.
She goes without complaint or fuss
In order to hear him say,
"I don't know who you are,
But I know I love you."

A Most Viable Widower

Have I got a woman for you!
—UBIQUITOUS

By the time he's back from the funeral, there's a pileup at his front door
    of covered dishes,
Filled with heat-and-eat meals and topped with notes full of heartfelt
    wishes to be of service to the grieving widower
Who will, before long, be neither grieving nor widower.

In good-enough health: new hip, a pacemaker, blood pressure under
    control, and sufficient sight
To keep on driving his car—even in winter! even at night!—plus financially
    secure and not bad-looking,
He is, we all agree, a most viable widower,

Able to walk a (slow) mile and to dance a (slow) dance, his mental
    faculties (mostly) okay,
And no grown children in rehab, unemployed, or planning to stay (maybe
    forever) down in the basement bedroom
Of the house of this oh-so-eligible widower,

Who's hearing, There's someone I want you to meet, and getting nonstop
    invitations to dinner,

And seated, yet again, beside another possible winner of the which-of-
   them-is-going-to-snag-him sweepstakes,
Clearly first prize among the available widowers.

And a little too soon he'll remarry, which is no sign of disrespect to his
   lost, late wife,
But because time's running out—he's in the November of his life, and
   because, in those sweet years they shared together,
He has learned how to be a husband, not a widower.

At the Japanese Restaurant

I am glad it cannot happen twice, the fever of first love.
—DAPHNE DU MAURIER

They are sitting side by side, not across from each other,
The better to lean, dissolve, melt into each other,
Hands lingering, eyes lingering on each other,
As they whisper, listen, nod, smile, laugh, and sigh,
And taste the offerings from each other's plate.
So in love. So newly in love. So wildly in love.

He is tucking a strand of hair behind her ear.
She is running a finger across his lower lip.
Hip pressed to each other's hip, they sip their wine,
Already hopelessly intoxicated.

Hello, young lovers.
We remember you,
Remember the feverish thrill of being you,
And find ourselves surprisingly contented
With where the years have brought us,
With not being crazed-with-love lovers anymore,
But an old, old married couple,
Here on the further, calmer shores of love,
Sharing, along with sashimi and a California roll,
A hot and sour, sweet and spicy life.

At the Playground

Just play. Have fun. Enjoy the game.
—MICHAEL JORDAN

That woman in the sundress and the sneakers
That woman with the hearing aid in her ear
That short-of-breath, red-of-face woman who is running here
    and there in the heavily humid ninety-plus-degrees heat
That woman who is somehow evading a skinny twelve-year-old boy,
And another who is going on fourteen,
As she sweatily dribbles the basketball
To the left,
To the right,
To the left,
To the right again
That woman who, though in urgent need of an air-conditioned room
    and a glass of iced tea,
Now aims
And jumps
And . . .
Fails to make the shot,
Her signature, underhand, nowhere-near-the-net shot,
Which brings her personal best to zero/fifteen
That fool-for-love woman who recklessly said yes to her two grandsons
    when they begged her to go to the playground with them to shoot
    hoops
That would be me.

Endings

Some of the Things That Are Not on My Bucket List

My advice to you is not to inquire why or whither, but just enjoy your ice cream while it's on your plate.
—THORNTON WILDER

I don't plan on fearlessly riding a camel across the desert sands.
I don't plan on running a marathon up in Boston.
I don't plan on reading M. Proust in French, nor do I have any plans
To be playing acoustic guitar in a bar down in Austin.

I don't plan on casting off manners and start saying whatever I please.
I don't plan on zipping on zip lines over abysses.
I don't plan on taking a course in conversational Japanese,
Or allowing myself to succumb to adulterous kisses.

I don't plan on being the oldest student at Harvard Medical School,
Or suiting up for some under-the-sea expedition.
I don't plan on piercing my labia, or places equally cool,
Or exploring the meaning of life in the lotus position.

I don't plan on writing a book that is unostentatiously profound.
I don't plan on getting into competitive rowing.
I just plan on planting some tulip bulbs, hoping to still be around
When the tulips start growing.

My Stuff

Keep the memories. Get rid of the stuff.
—REAL ESTATE AGENT

The trouble is I really love my stuff,
Especially the stuff that's stashed in my basement,
Like that trunkful of 78s that I haven't listened to in over seventy years,
When the Andrews Sisters sang "Rum and Coca Cola,"
And Sinatra sang "Full Moon and Empty Arms,"
And I forget who sang "Chattanooga Choo Choo,"
All of them played on what we called a Victrola
In the sun parlor—always my childhood's favorite room,
Where built-in shelves held my Oz books, *The Secret Garden*,
The Count of Monte Cristo, the Nancy Drews,
All of them also safely stashed in the basement
Of the house I live in now, and am leaving now,
Except—how can I leave without my stuff?

Lunch With Shirley

The living moment is everything.
—D. H. LAWRENCE

So sometimes I wake in the morning and I'm thinking
That this could turn out to be my last day on earth,
So I'd better start savoring every precious moment,
Every single precious, blessed moment,
Each and every relentlessly precious, relentlessly
        blessed moment
Of what could turn out to be my last day on earth.

This is very exhausting.

So I'm thinking today I'll just have lunch with Shirley,
And we'll share the Caesar salad and the shrimp,
And talk, through our decaf espressos, about everything
        and nothing, nothing and everything:
Our marriages, thinning hair, gun control, the grandchildren.
How many times we get up to pee at night.
The coming election, our book-club selection, whether this
        lipstick's too bright.
And does eating a pickle really help with leg cramps.

We'll bitch a little and laugh a lot and gossip more than we should,
Trusting there's nothing it isn't safe to say.
And I'm thinking that lunch with Shirley on an ordinary day
Would not be a bad way to spend my last day on earth.

My Father, the Age I Am Now

Time, which diminishes all things, increases
understanding for the aging.
—PLUTARCH

My mother was the star:
Smart and funny and warm,
A patient listener and an easy laugher.
My father was . . . an accountant:
Not one to look up to,
Ask advice from,
Confide in.
A man of few words.

We faulted him—my mother, my sister, and I,
For being this dutiful, uninspiring guy
Who never missed a day of work,
Or wondered what our dreams were.
Just . . . an accountant.

Decades later,
My mother dead, my sister dead,
My father, the age I am now,
Planning ahead in his so-accountant way,
Sent me, for my records,

Copies of his will, his insurance policies,
And assorted other documents, including
The paid receipt for his cemetery plot,
The paid receipt for his tombstone,
And the words that he had chosen for his stone.

And for the first time, shame on me, I saw my father:
Our family's prime provider, only provider.
A barely-out-of-boyhood married man
Working without a safety net through the Depression years
That marked him forever,
Terrified that maybe he wouldn't make it,
Terrified he would fall and drag us down with him,
His only goal, his life-consuming goal,
To put bread on our table, a roof over our head.

With no time for anyone's secrets,
With no time for anyone's dreams,
He quietly earned the words that made me weep,
The words that were carved, the following year,
On his tombstone:
HE TOOK CARE OF HIS FAMILY.

The Remains of the Day

May you live every day of your life.
—JONATHAN SWIFT

It's okay to find your missing keys
In the pocket of your raincoat.
It's not so okay to find them in the freezer,
Which means as of now I am definitely okay.
And having considered all that is gone,
And compared it with all that remains,
I've decided that I definitely want to stay
A little, or maybe even a whole lot, longer.

I've still got several new sunsets to see,
And more gourmet meat loafs to make.
There are those, and they know who they are,
Who still need my advice.
I'd want to keep hugging my family.
I'd want to keep drinking a good Chardonnay.
And finally losing those damn seven pounds
        would be nice.

I'd still be reading the papers, and still hollering
    at the TV,
Still hoping for better days and for better news.
"Mellow" would be an adjective rarely applicable
    to me.
"Diffident" wouldn't describe me expressing my
    views.

And if there should come a time when my grand-
    daughter finds my keys in the freezer,
That won't necessarily mean that I'm fatally old.
Some people, I'd tell her, keep their keys in the
    pocket of their raincoat.
I prefer to keep my keys very cold.

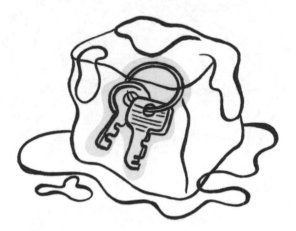

Not Especially Spiritual

It is one of the blessings of old friends that you can
afford to be stupid with them.
—RALPH WALDO EMERSON

When my oldest friend Phyllis was dying I went to visit her,
Holding her hand as I sat by her hospice bed.
Is there anything final, I asked, that we should be talking about?
Probably not, she answered, shaking her head.
Why don't we just forget about final anythings
And count the number of guys we've slept with instead?
So we laughed, sighed, cringed, and counted our way up to
—How many? None of your business!—till we were done.
Not especially spiritual, but such fun.

Answers

In the book of life, the answers aren't in the back.

—CHARLIE BROWN

I do not believe in God,
But if I did,
I might be thinking he's not such a lovely person,
Considering all the misery and injustice in this world,
Some of which (volcanoes and earthquakes, for instance),
Cannot, in spite of free will, including
Our freedom to screw things up,
Be blamed on us.
Furthermore, I do not believe in an Afterlife
With a downstairs and upstairs for the naughty and nice,
Our room assignments made by a Higher Authority
Whose job has been to scare us into behaving ourselves.
On the other hand, I do believe in Mystery,
And in my inability to fathom
How the world came into being,
How life began,
And, if there is a point,
The point of it all.
So if you are looking for answers from this old lady,
You won't find them here.

A Warning (or Maybe a Love Song) for My Husband

... till death do us part.
—TRADITIONAL WEDDING VOW

Each morning I get up before you
And stand by your side of the bed.
I'm checking your chest to make sure you
Are breathing. Still breathing. Not dead.
The reason I worry about you
Is widowhood's *not* my Plan D.
I don't intend living without you.
So don't you dare die before me.

Of course you're a pain in the ass, dear.
Go show me a husband who's not.
But on all the others I'll pass, dear,
And stick with the guy that I've got.
And yes, we have what are called issues,
Not always resolved peaceably.
But spare me the tears and the tissues.
Don't you dare die before me.

My words aren't meant to disparage
Those ladies who live on their own.
But after six decades of marriage,
I'd rather not go it alone.
The sentiment here may not thrill you,
But listen, my love, carefully:
Keep staying alive, or I'll kill you.
Don't you dare die before me.

Attitude

People are not disturbed by things, but by
the view they take of them.
—EPICTETUS

Once upon a time I flirted,
Smooth of skin, long-haired, tight-skirted,
Never satisfied with what I got.
Foolish choices. Duds I dated.
Bad vacations. Jobs I hated.
What did I complain about? A lot.

Once upon a time I twinkled.
Now I'm achy, creaky, crinkled,
Also slowed-down, sidelined, out of touch.
No stroke. No chemotherapy.
And (as of now) dementia-free.
What's there to complain about? Not much.

Another Way of Looking at Things

Humankind cannot bear very much reality.
—T. S. ELIOT

When they told me you were dead,
I chose not to believe them,
Imagining instead that you were away,
Gone on a windy business trip to Chicago,
Taking in an opera at Santa Fe,
Up in Woods Hole doing something marine biological,
Vacationing on lobster rolls in Maine,
Or even that you had packed up and moved
To the other side of the world,
Where maybe I might never see you again,
Except that I could
I could
I could,
If I really needed to.

Lasts

I want all of my lasts to be with you.

—ANONYMOUS

Wouldn't I linger with you till the sky had turned black
If this was the very last sunset we'd ever see?
Wouldn't desire be trumping that pain in my back
If this was the last time that you could make love to me?
Would I complain you were stepping all over my toes
If this was the last of the dances we'd ever dance?
And wouldn't I travel wherever the highway goes,
If you traveled with me and this was our last chance?

My Legacy

Promise me you'll never forget me because if I thought
you would, I'd never leave.
—WINNIE-THE-POOH

Since it's looking as if my legacy isn't shaping up to be
Peace on earth and universal health care,
Here's what I'm hoping to be remembered for:

Showing up when I say I'm showing up.
Sticking with what I've started until it's done.
Sending valentines to all the children in our family (until they
        reach the age of twenty-one).
And never, ever leaving the house without eyeliner.

Playing a relentless game of Scrabble.
Keeping the secrets I promised I would keep.
Being able to laugh about the bad things that happen to me
(Though not before I first whine, and weep, and rail against
        my fate, and blame my husband).

Doing work I'm able to be proud of.
Making a truly transcendent matzoh ball.
Coming to terms with mortality (though, to be perfectly honest,
I'm still not feeling all that thrilled about dying).

Coming to terms with not feeling thrilled about dying.

Watching over the people that I love.
(Grateful they're watching over me as well.)
Enjoying whatever there is to enjoy until that final, time's-up,
        closing bell.
And hoping—just a reminder—that I'll be remembered.

About the Author

JUDITH VIORST was born and brought up in New Jersey, graduated from Rutgers University, moved to Greenwich Village, and has lived in Washington, D.C., since 1960, when she married Milton Viorst, a political writer. They have three sons and seven grandchildren. A 1981 graduate of the Washington Psychoanalytic Institute, Viorst writes in many different areas: science books; children's picture books—including the beloved *Alexander and the Terrible, Horrible, No Good, Very Bad Day*; adult fiction and nonfiction—including the bestselling *Necessary Losses*; poetry for children and adults; and musical theater.

Quotes from Judith Viorst's Decade Books

THIRTY

It's true love because . . .
When he is late for dinner and I know he must be either having
    an affair or lying dead in the middle of the street,
I always hope he's dead.

FORTY

When, instead of vice versa,
Did I start to pick investments over adventure,
And clean over scenic, and comfortable over intense?
Why does a relationship
Between an older woman and younger man
Suddenly seem to make a lot of sense?

FIFTY

Before I go, I'd like to have high cheekbones.
I'd like to talk less like New Jersey, and more like
    Claire Bloom.
And whenever I enter a room, I'd like an orchestra
    to burst into my theme song.
I'd like to have a theme song before I go.

SIXTY

I've reached the stage where a lot of the reading I'm doing is at the
    market checking salt-free and fat-free and expiration dates. . . .
And when I have to admit that, offered the choice, I'd—unhesitatingly—
    give up a night of wild rapture with Denzel Washington
For a nice report on my next bone density test,
I know that I have reached a whole other stage.

SEVENTY

They may be middle-aged, but they're still my children,
And even though they think they don't need my advice,
They need it.
Because who else is going to tell them:
Check your moles once a year with the dermatologist. . . .
And . . . shave off the mustache—it makes you look like Hitler.

EIGHTY

He knows when he goes for his CAT scan that I'll gladly take him.
I know when I go for some blood work he'll come and he'll wait.
These are not like those torrid times on that beach in New Jersey,
But a date is a date.

More from bestselling author
JUDITH VIORST